WH S

STS
actice papers

FOR THE YEAR 2002

AGE
10-11
Key Stage 2

Maths

Book 2 Levels 3-6

practice Papers

Contents

First published 2001
exclusively for WHSmith by

Hodder & Stoughton Educational,
a division of Hodder Headline Ltd
338 Euston Road
London NW1 3BH

A CIP record for this book is available from the British Library.

Authors: Steve Mills and Hilary Koll

ISBN 0340 84607 0

Printed and bound by Graphycems, Spain

NOTE: The tests, questions and advice in this book are not reproductions of the official test materials sent to schools. The official testing process is supported by guidance and training for teachers in setting and marking tests and interpreting the results. The results achieved in the tests in this book may not be the same as are achieved in the official tests.

THE NATIONAL TESTS: A SUMMARY

What are the National Tests?

Children who attend state schools in England and Wales sit National Tests (SATs) at the ages of 7, 11 and 14, usually at the beginning of May. They may also sit optional tests in the intervening years – many schools have chosen to adopt these tests. The test results are accompanied by an assessment by the child's teacher.

The results are used by the school to assess each child's level of knowledge and progress in English and Maths at Key Stage 1 and English, Maths and Science at Key Stages 2 and 3. They also provide useful guidance for the child's next teacher.

The educational calendar for children aged 5–14 is structured as follows:

Key Stage	Year	Age by end of year	National Test
1 (KS1)	1	6	
	2	7	KEY STAGE 1
2 (KS2)	3	8	Optional Year 3
	4	9	Optional Year 4
	5	10	Optional Year 5
	6	11	KEY STAGE 2
3 (KS3)	7	12	
	8	13	
	9	14	KEY STAGE 3

Test timetable

The Key Stage 1 National Tests are carried out in **May**.

Key Stage 2 tests take place in one week in May. All children sit the same test at the same time. In 2002, the tests will take place in the week of **13–17 May**. Your child's school will be able to provide you with a detailed timetable.

Key Stage 3 students will sit their tests on **7–13 May**.

Levels

National average levels have been set for children's results in the National Tests. The levels are as follows:

LEVEL	AGE 7 (Key Stage 1)	AGE 11 (Key Stage 2)	AGE 14 (Key Stage 3)
8			
7			
6			
5			
4			
3			
2			
2a			
2b			
2c			
1			

- BELOW EXPECTED LEVEL
- EXPECTED LEVEL
- ABOVE EXPECTED LEVEL
- EXCEPTIONAL

Results

Your child's school will send you a report indicating his or her levels in the tests and the teacher assessment.

The school's overall test results will be included in local and national league tables, which are published in most newspapers.

What can parents do to help?

While it is never a good idea to encourage cramming, you can help your child to succeed by:

- Making sure he or she has enough food, sleep and leisure time during the test period.
- Practising important skills such as writing and reading stories, spelling and mental arithmetic.
- Telling him or her what to expect in the test, such as important symbols and key words.
- Helping him or her to be comfortable in test conditions including working within a time limit, reading questions carefully and understanding different ways of answering.

MATHS at Key Stage 2

The Key Stage 2 National Tests cover Number, Measures, Shape and Space and Data Handling. Most children will take two one-hour written tests and a short, orally delivered mental test. Test A is a written non-calculator paper and Test B is a written paper where children can use a calculator, should they wish. There is also a written extension test, Test C, that some more able children might be given.

Levels

Children taking the Mathematics Tests A and B and the mental mathematics test can achieve below level 3, level 3, level 4 or level 5, with a typical 11-year-old attaining level 4. For a child attaining a very high score, a further test (Test C) can be given to ascertain whether he or she is performing at level 6.

To gain an idea of the level at which your child is working, use the table on page 36, which shows you how to convert your child's marks into a National Curriculum level.

Setting the tests

Allow one hour for each of the written tests. Do not expect your child to take them one after another. In the National Test week, children will take the mathematics tests over two or three days.

For the written tests, your child will need a ruler, pencil, rubber, protractor and, if possible, a small mirror or piece of tracing paper, together with a calculator (for Tests B and C).

The mental test should take approximately 10–15 minutes to give, and it is necessary for you to read aloud the questions on pages 27–28, which you should cut out for ease of use. Your child will only need a pencil and rubber for the mental test.

Written tests A and B

Allow one hour for each of these tests. Encourage your child to work systematically through each test, returning later to questions which cause difficulty.

If your child has difficulty in reading the questions, you can read them aloud, provided the mathematical words are not altered or explained. Where necessary, your child can dictate their answers and these can be written down for him or her. For large numbers, however, your child should be clear which digits are intended to be written, e.g. for a number such as three thousand and six your child should indicate that this is written as three, zero, zero, six.

The Mental Maths Test

The mental test contains a series of questions for you to read to your child together with sheets for written answers. Allow only the time suggested for each question, reading each one twice.

Marking the tests

Next to each question in the written tests is a number indicating how many marks the question or part of the question is worth. Enter your child's mark into the circle above, using the answer pages to help you decide how many points to award.

Find your child's total score from the written tests and mental test and refer to page 36 for information about the level your child might be working at.

Test C

If your child achieves level 5, he or she can try Test C (on pages 37–42), to ascertain whether he or she is working at level 6. Allow 40 minutes for this test and provide your child with a calculator to use where necessary.

1 Fill in the missing numbers.

$24 \div$ [4] $= 6$

1

$38 - 15 = 39 -$ [16]

1

$(5 \times 6) - 15 = 10 +$ [5]

1

2 Arrange these numbers in **order of size**, starting with the smallest.

911 375 824 359 602

(359) (375) (602) (824) (911)

smallest

1

3 Arrange these four number cards to make a **subtraction** question with an **answer** of **67**.

[8] [2] **–** [1] [5] **= 67**

1

TOTAL

5

4 Jack goes to the cinema with two friends. He buys **three** tickets that are all the same price.

He pays with a **£5 note** and is given **50p change.**

How much does **one** ticket cost?

2

2

TOTAL

4

5 Draw a ring around the **three** numbers that when **divided by 4** leave no remainder.

27 48 34 29 88 200

6 Claire is looking at a list of some **prime time** television programmes. **Prime time** is between 6 p.m. and 9 p.m.

Prime time TV

	Channel 1	**Channel 2**	**Channel 3**
6.00	News	Cartoon	Film ↓
6.30	Comedy	Quiz show	
7.00	Football ↓	Cookery show	
7.30		Drama ↓	Documentary
8.00			News
8.30		Wildlife show	Weather

Claire turns on the TV to Channel 2 at **twenty five to seven.** What is showing?

1

Claire watches Channel 2 for **30 minutes** and then turns over to Channel 3.

What is showing on Channel 3?

1

The football programme on Channel 1 starts at 7.00 and lasts for **130 minutes.**

What time does it end?

1

TOTAL

3

7 This is a spinner on a TV game show.

The contestants spin the pointer to see what prize they will win. The spinner is a regular octagon.

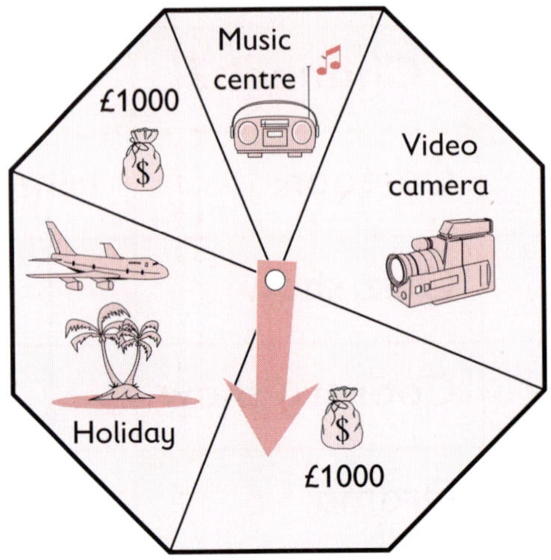

A contestant spins the pointer.

Which prize is the contestant **most likely** to win?

1

What is the **probability** of winning the music centre?

Give your answer as a fraction.

1

Jo says '*The probability of winning a holiday is* $\frac{1}{4}$'

Rob says '*The probability of winning a holiday is* $\frac{2}{8}$'

Explain who you think is telling the truth and why.

1

TOTAL

3

8 A factory has made some sinks with unusually shaped plug-holes.

Three different plug-holes are shown with their plugs.

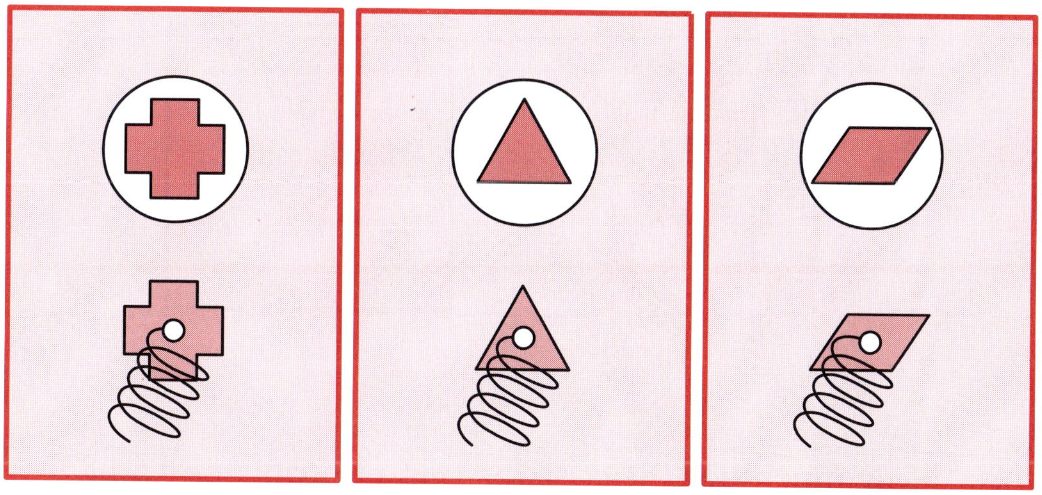

Each plug will fit into its plug-hole in more than one way.

Write how many different ways each plug can fit.

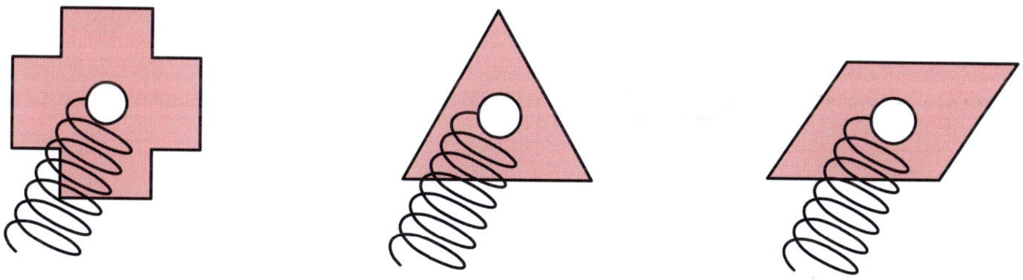

2

9 Calculate

906 – 245

1

TOTAL

3

10 The cost of developing **24** photographs is **£7.20**.

Photo developing:

24 for £7.20

How much does it cost for one photograph to be developed?

2

11 Calculate

$$21 \times 542$$

2

TOTAL

4

12 Kevin has been keeping a record of temperatures in Stalywell, at 6 a.m. on the first day of the month between January and July.

Here is his record.

	Temperature in Stalywell
January 1st	−11°C
February 1st	−8°C
March 1st	−1°C
April 1st	4°C
May 1st	9°C
June 1st	17°C
July 1st	23°C

What is the difference between the temperatures recorded in January and May?

□ °C

How many degrees colder was it on February 1st than April 1st?

□ °C

Which two temperatures in the table have a difference of 17°C?

□ °C □ °C

The temperature on December 1st was 2°C colder than in January. What was the temperature on December 1st?

□ °C

1

1

1

1

TOTAL

4

13 Here is a plan of a garden. A gardener wants to dig a pond to cover **20%** of the garden.

Shade an area that is **20%** of the whole garden.

The pond can be any shape.

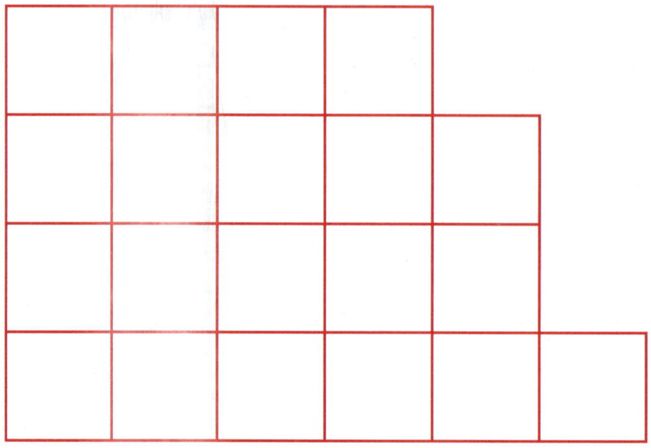

1

The garden has an **area** of **80 square metres**.

What is the **area** of the pond?

$\square$ m^2

1

14 Graham is describing one of these statements.

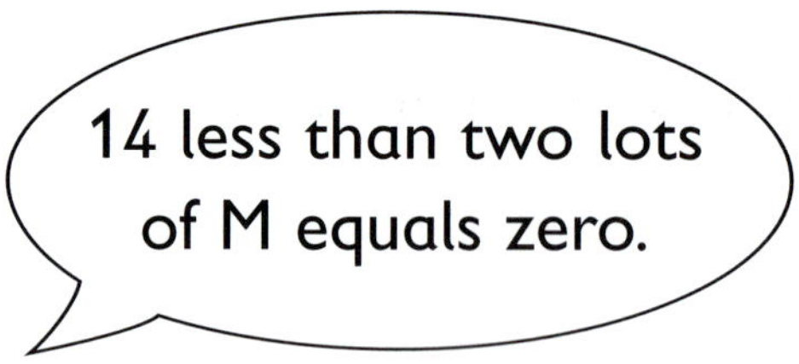

Circle which of these statements he is describing.

$14 - 2M = 0$ $2M - 14 = 0$

$14 - M + 2 = 0$ $M \times M - 14 = 0$

1

TOTAL

3

15 Here is a map of a safari park.

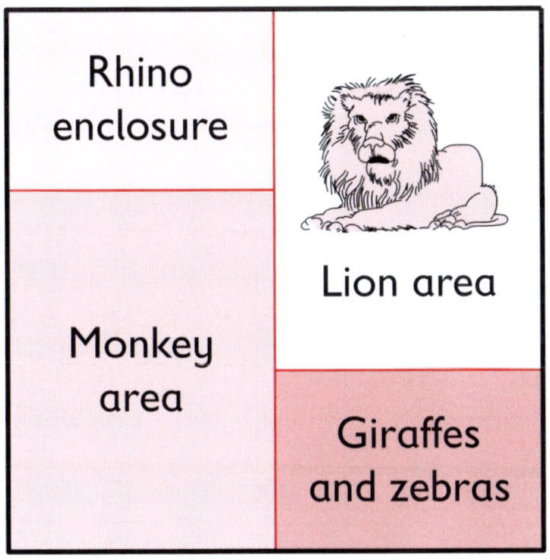

Approximately what **fraction** of the park does the **lion area** cover?

1

The safari park is in the shape of a **square**. The **length** of one side of the square is **3 km**.

What is the **perimeter** of the park?

1

16 **Two** numbers in the grid below have a total of 1.
Circle both numbers.

0.31	0.62	0.2
0.98	0.45	0.09
0.55	0.1	0.7

1

TOTAL

3

17 Here is a grid made of squares. One **eighth** of the grid has been shaded.

Shade an extra **quarter** of the grid so that one eighth and one quarter are shaded.

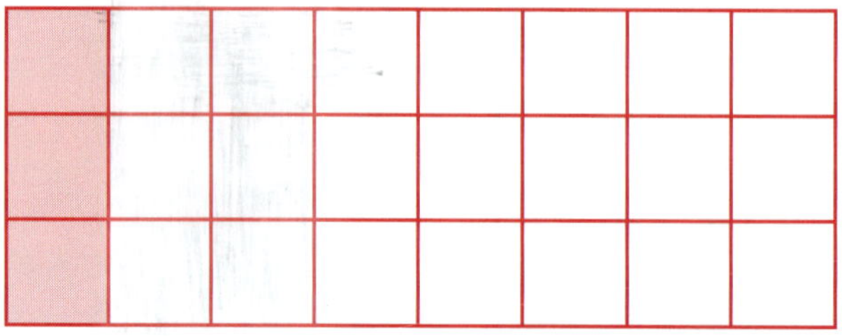

1

What fraction of the whole grid is now shaded?

1

18 The minute hand on this clock is pointing to the number 3.

How many **degrees** will it turn clockwise to point to the number **12**?

1

Starting at the number 3, which **number** will the minute hand point to after a clockwise turn of **60°**?

1

TOTAL

4

19 This table shows what 6 children had in their lunchbox on Monday.

Name	Drink	Roll	Chocolate	Crisps
Kim	1	2	0	1
Ali	1	1	1	0
Jo	1	0	2	1
Dev	0	2	2	1
Sam	1	1	0	1
Kate	1	3	1	0

This chart shows what **5** of the children had in their lunchbox. **One child's** information has been missed off this chart.

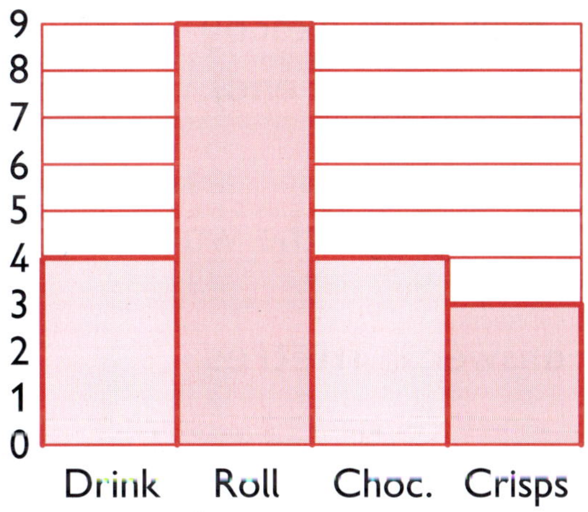

Which child's information has been missed off this chart?

1

Explain how you worked this out.

1

TOTAL

2

20 Here is part of a wall made from two layers of bricks. The bricks on the top row are arranged so that their ends are exactly **half way** along the bricks on the bottom row.

At each end of the top row is half a brick to complete the wall.

The whole bricks are 20 cm in length.

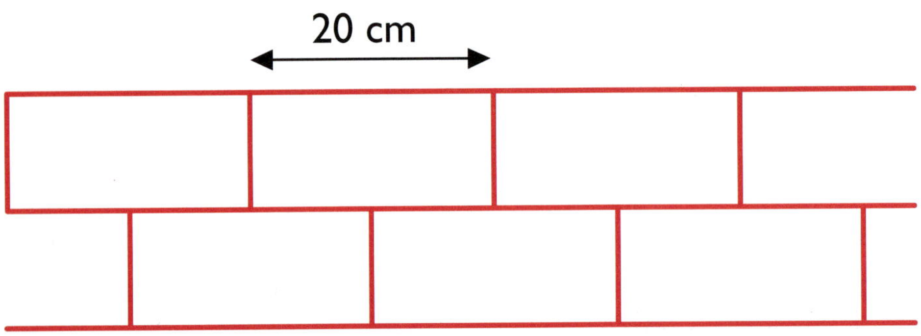

The wall is built from exactly **19** whole bricks and two half bricks (one at each end).

What is the **length** of the wall?

Give your answer in **metres**.

m

2

TOTAL

2

1 Fill in the **missing numbers** to make the number sentences correct.

☐ − 48 = 99 — 1

17 × ☐ = 527 — 1

☐ ÷ ☐ = 12 — 1

2 **Two** of the numbers below have a **total** of **100**.

47	50	18
25	63	81
82	36	85

Write the two numbers here.

◯ ◯ — 1

TOTAL 4

3 Mrs Gulfaraz is a nurse.

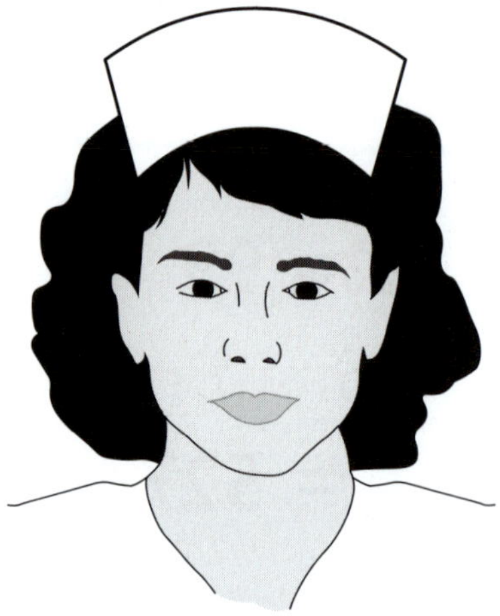

She works **44** hours every week.

She is paid **£6.95** for each **hour**.

How much money does she get paid every week?

£

1

Mrs Gulfaraz needs **£500** to buy a small car.

What is the least number of **hours** she will have to work to be paid **£500**?

2

TOTAL

3

4 This quadrilateral has three equal sides and a longer side.

Measure **accurately** the **longest** side in **millimetres**.

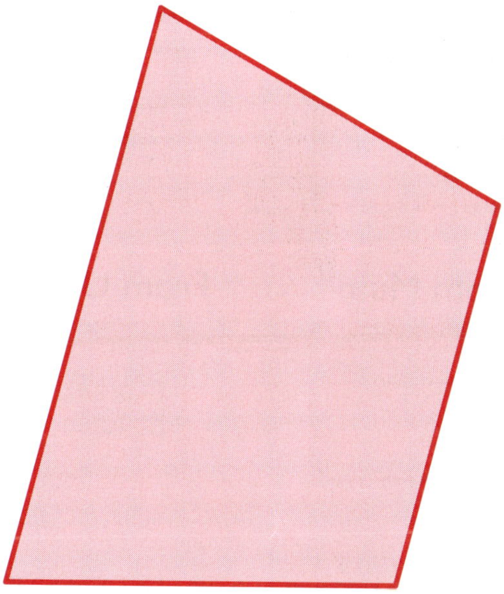

mm

1

5 Sam is holding a picture of some shapes.

He holds the picture and looks in a mirror.

Draw how the shapes would look in the mirror.

2

TOTAL

3

6 It is Molly's birthday. She has been sent **six** cards in identical envelopes.

Molly closes her eyes and picks **one** envelope to open.

What is the **probability** that she chooses the card from **Granny**?

Write your answer as a fraction.

1

What is the **probability** that she chooses a card from **a man**?

Write your answer as a fraction in its **simplest form**.

2

TOTAL

3

7 These two number cards are face down on a table.

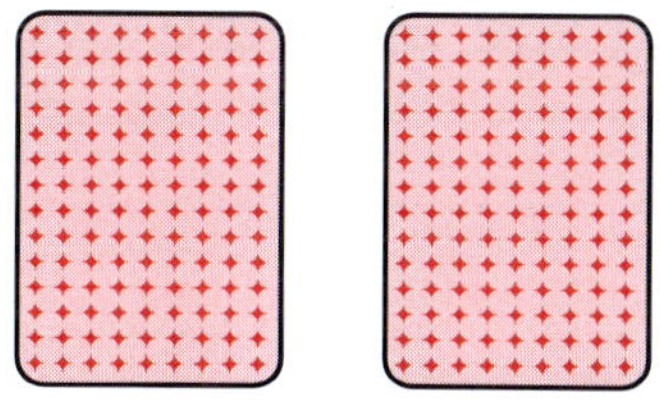

One card has a number **greater than zero.**

The other card has a number **less than zero.**

The **difference** between the two numbers on the cards is **6.**

Write what the two numbers could be.

1

8 This list gives the distances of some cities from Manchester.

The distances are given in **miles.**

Distance from Manchester in miles	
London	192
Birmingham	81
Glasgow	210
Liverpool	50
Aberdeen	332

James travelled from **London** to **Manchester** and then on from **Manchester** to **another city**.

He travelled **402 miles** in total.

Which other city did he travel to?

1

TOTAL

2

9 Mrs Taylor is doing some cooking.

During the morning she uses the oven to bake some cakes.

This chart shows the temperature inside her oven at different times in the morning.

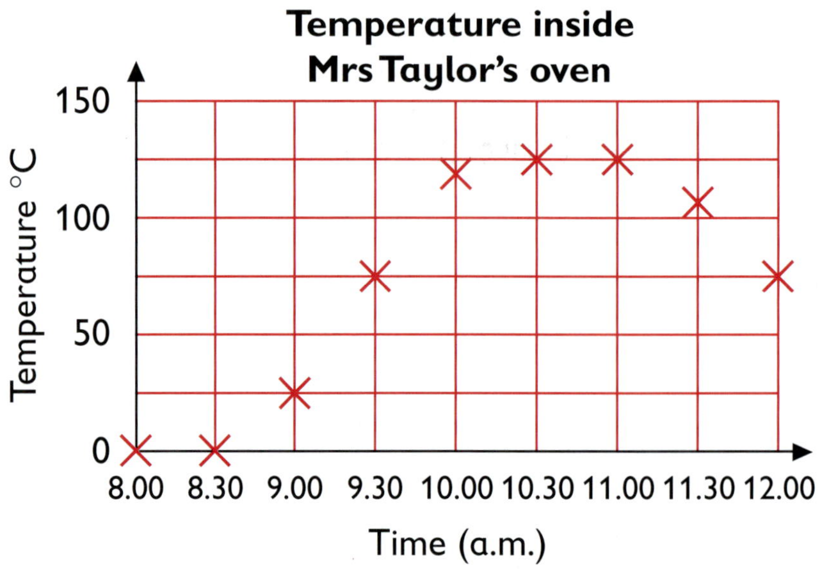

Between which two times did Mrs Taylor turn the oven on?

Between [ ] and [ ]

1

What was the approximate temperature at 10 a.m.?

[ ]

1

For how long was the oven hotter than 75°C?

Give your answer in minutes.

[ ]

1

TOTAL

3

10 In a P.E. lesson a class of children is working in teams of **5.**

There are **3 girls** and **2 boys** in every team.

There are **14 boys** in the class.

How many girls are there?

2

11 Fill in the missing digits to make these number sentences correct.

$\square\square \times \square = 399$

1

$4\square\square \div \square = 90$

1

TOTAL

4

12 Sarah wants to hang a painting on her wall between two shelves.

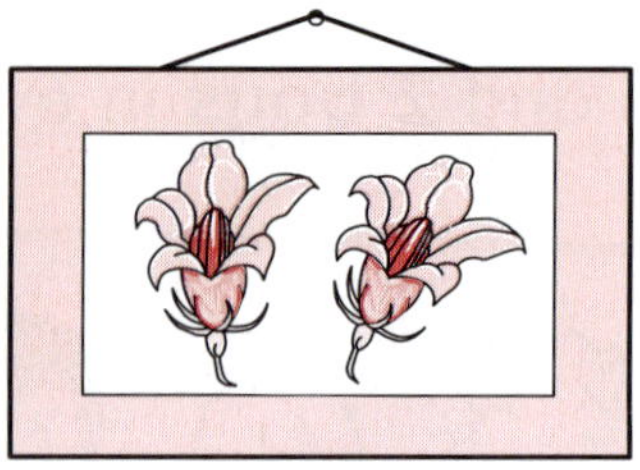

One shelf is **86 cm** from the floor.

The other shelf is **180 cm** from the floor.

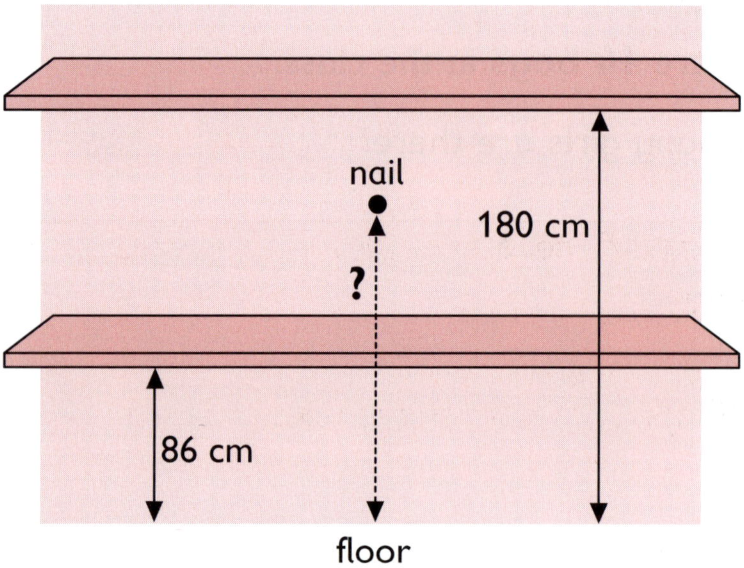

Sarah puts the nail **exactly half way** between the two shelves.

How many **centimetres** from the floor does she put the nail?

2

TOTAL

2

13 Look at the shapes on the grid.

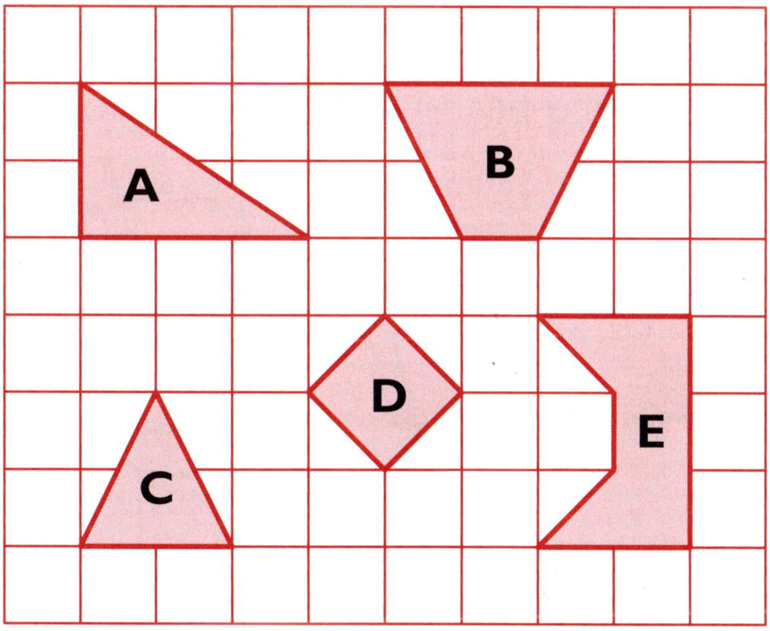

Write **one** of the letters into each sentence to make it correct.

Shape ☐ is an isosceles triangle. 1

Shape ☐ is a regular shape. 1

Shape ☐ does not have reflective symmetry. 1

14 Calculate

$$\frac{5}{8} \text{ of } 792$$

☐ 1

TOTAL 4

15 A fast food restaurant sells **Merry Meals.**

A **Merry Meal** contains:

a **120 g** burger, **75 g** fries and **300 ml** cola:

120 g 75 g 300 ml

Rakeeb bought some **Merry Meals** for his family.

They did not eat everything.

Altogether his family ate **425 g** of fries and drank **over a litre and a half** of cola.

What is the smallest number of **Merry Meals** Rakeeb could have bought?

2

1

TOTAL

3

16 Fill in the missing number.

$894.6 \div \square = 42.6$

17 A picture of a bus has been reflected and rotated on this grid.

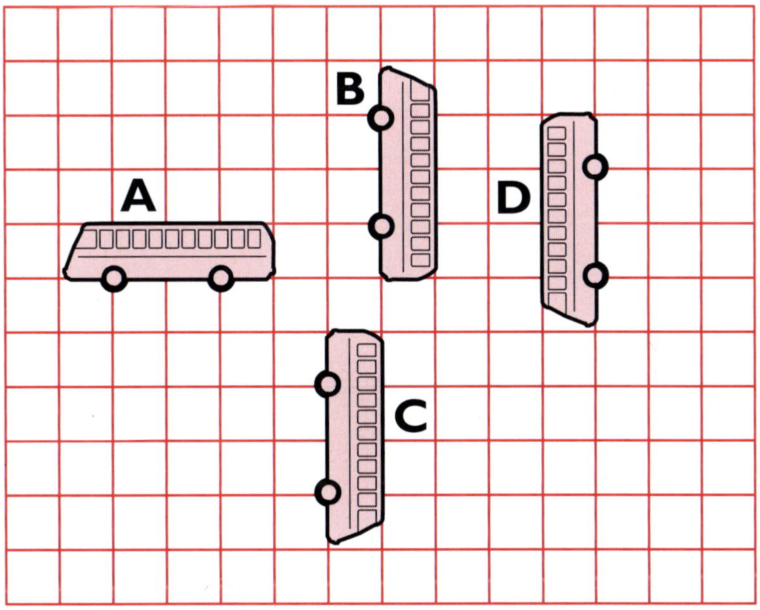

Write the letter of the bus that is a **reflection** of bus **A**.

Bus A is **rotated through two right angles** about the **point P**.

Draw the outline of the rotated shape on the grid below.

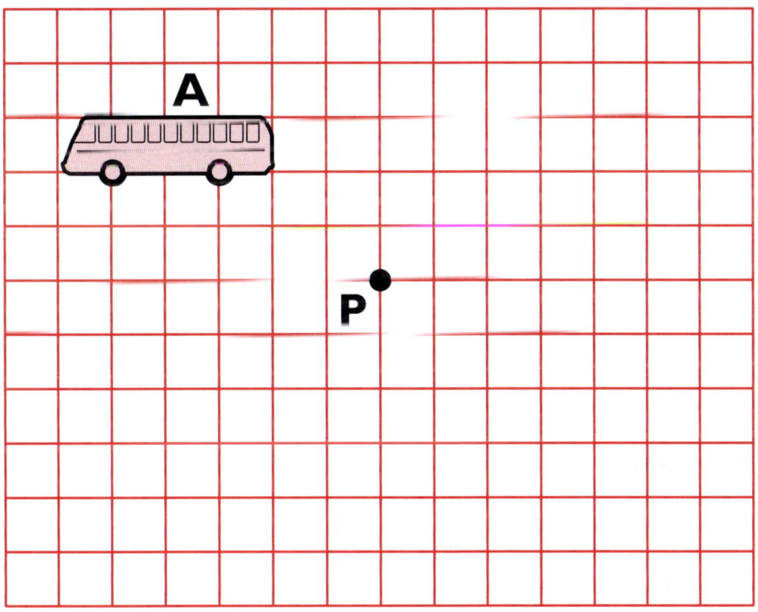

1

2

TOTAL

3

18 Daniel has started to draw an **equilateral triangle**, with sides **10 cm** long. He has drawn one of the sides.

Finish drawing the **equilateral triangle.**

Use an angle measurer (protractor) and a ruler.

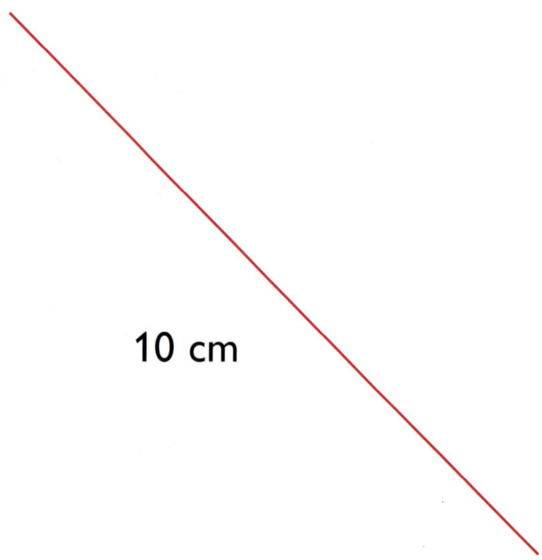

2

1

19 Calculate

17% of £204

TOTAL

3

20 Andy and Chloe threw stones into the sea.

This graph shows the **height** that their stones went before falling into the sea.

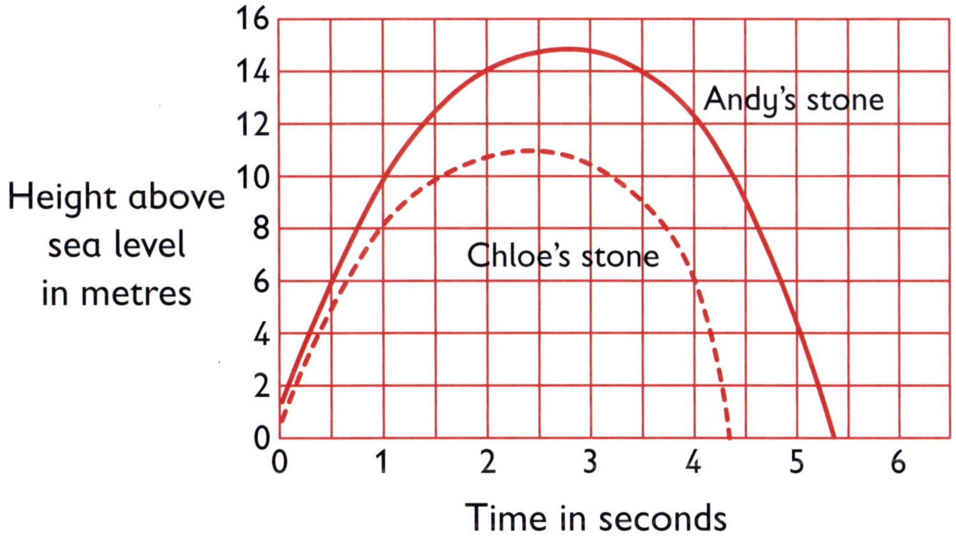

Approximately how many seconds after Chloe's stone fell into the sea did Andy's stone fall in?

1

After how many seconds was Andy's stone twice as high as Chloe's?

1

Sanjay is looking at the graph. He says:

"The graph is wrong. The curves do not start at 0 metres."

Explain in words why you think that the curves do **not** start at the bottom of the graph.

1

TOTAL

3

Mental Maths Test

Answer Sheet

5-second questions

1		4	
2		5	
3		6	ml

6

10-second questions

7	degrees	12	weeks
8	31, 12	13	2 4 7 11 ?
9		14	minutes
10	metres	15	$\frac{10}{4}$ $\frac{40}{100}$ $\frac{3}{8}$ $\frac{2}{5}$
11	$x =$ $36 - x = 27$		

9

15-second questions

16	Jo 58 metres Dev 24 metres Sanjay 29 metres Chris 104 metres	18	3.7 4.52 5.1 3.99 2.3
		19	£
17		20	6 10 12 60 5

5

TOTAL

20

"For this first set of questions you have five seconds to work out each answer and write it down."

1 What is double forty five?

2 What is thirty eight less than fifty?

3 Write the number twenty thousand three hundred and four in figures.

4 Two green cubes and three white cubes are in a bag. The probability of picking a green cube is two fifths. What is the probability of picking a white cube?

5 What is forty eight divided by eight?

6 How many millilitres are there in three and a half litres?

"For the next set of questions you have ten seconds to work out each answer and write it down."

7 How many degrees do the four angles of a square add up to?

8 What is the difference between thirty one and twelve?

9 Multiply six by four and then subtract seven.

10 What is two hundred and thirty nine centimetres to the nearest metre?

11 Look at the answer sheet. In the equation, what is the value of x?

12 Paul cycles six miles a week. In how many weeks will he have cycled forty two miles?

13 Look at the answer sheet. What is the next number in the sequence?

14 A film started at quarter to nine. It finished at ten o'clock. How many minutes did the film last?

15 Look at the answer sheet. Draw a ring around two fractions equivalent to four tenths.

"For the next set of questions you have fifteen seconds to work out each answer and write it down."

16 Look at the answer sheet. Here are some distances thrown in the javelin. Draw a ring round the person who threw the javelin half as far as Jo.

17 Seventy five per cent of a number is eighteen. What is the number?

18 Look at the answer sheet. Draw a ring around the largest number.

19 I went to the shop with two pounds. I spent forty one pence and then fifty three pence. How much did I have left?

20 Look at the answer sheet. Draw a ring around any of the numbers that are factors of thirty.

Answers
Test A

Question number	Answer	Mark	Parent's notes and additional comments
1a	4	1	
1b	16	1	
1c	5	1	
2	359, 375, 602, 824, 911	1	The numbers must be written from smallest to largest.
3	82 – 15	1	
4	£1.50 *or* 150p Award one mark for workings that show £4.50 ÷ 3, but with an incorrect answer	2	Note that amounts of money should never be written with both the **£** sign and a **p** sign, e.g. £1.50p is incorrect and would not earn a mark.
5	48, 88, 200	2	Award 1 mark only if only two are correctly identified.
6a	Quiz show	1	Children will benefit from practice in reading and interpreting TV schedules.
6b	Film	1	30 minutes after 6:35 is 7:05. A film is showing on Channel 3 at this time.
6c	9.10 *or* 9.10 p.m. *or* 21:10	1	130 minutes is 2 hours and 10 minutes. Encourage children to practise converting from minutes to hours and vice versa.
7a	£1000 *or* 'money'	1	Children are required to notice that there are two sections showing £1000, which together cover a greater area than the other prizes.
7b	$\frac{1}{8}$	1	Children should notice that the spinner can be divided into 8 sections and that one of the sections has the music centre prize. Thus the probability is one out of 8. Probabilities generally can be written in words or as fractions or decimals, e.g. **one out of four, $\frac{1}{4}$ or 0.25**
7c	Both are telling the truth. Explanations must make reference to the fact that $\frac{2}{8}$ is the same as $\frac{1}{4}$	1	These two fractions are 'equivalent' meaning that they have the same value, e.g. if you have $\frac{2}{8}$ of a pizza it is the same value as $\frac{1}{4}$ of a pizza. 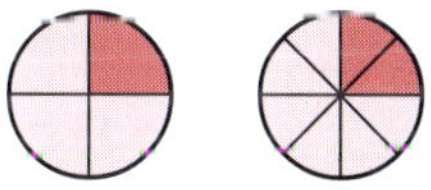
8	4, 3, 2 Award one mark if two out of the three answers are correct.	2	
9	661	1	
10	30p or £0.30 Award one mark if workings show an attempt to divide 720 by 24, but with an incorrect answer.	2	Children can answer this question using any method. Encourage your child to make a mental approximation, e.g. 720 is about 700 and 24 is about 25. 700 ÷ 25 is 28, so the answer will be about 28. This can help children to avoid unnecessary errors.

Test A Answers

Question number	Answer	Mark	Parent's notes and additional comments
11	11382 Award one mark for attempts to multiply 20 by 542 and 1 by 542, and adding the parts together, in whatever form, e.g. $\begin{array}{r} 542 \\ \times\ 20 \\ \hline 10840 \\ +\ 542 \\ \hline \end{array}$ incorrect answer *or* $10 \times 542 = 5420$ $+\ 10 \times 542 = 5420$ $+\ 1 \times 542 = \underline{542}$ incorrect answer	2	Children can answer this question using any non-calculator method. Encourage your child to make a mental approximation, e.g. 21 is about 20 and 542 is about 500. 20×500 is 10000, so the answer will be about 10000. This can help children to avoid unnecessary errors, e.g. giving answers such as 1626.
12a	20°C	1	Encourage your child to draw or imagine a number line from −11 to 9 and to count from −11 to zero (= 11) and from zero to 9 (= 9) and to find the total.
12b	12°C	1	Again, encourage your child to draw or imagine a number line, this time from −8 to 4 and to count back from 4 to zero (=4) and from zero to −8 (=8) and to find the total.
12c	−8°C, 9°C *or* 9°C, −8°C	1	
12d	−13°C	1	Children often make errors in counting on or back starting from a negative number. With positive numbers, 11 − 2 = 9. With negative numbers, e.g. −11 − 2 is not −9 but −13.
13a	An area of 4 squares should be shaded. These can be made from part squares provided the total number of squares shaded is 4.	1	There are 20 squares in the plan of the garden. 20% of 20 is 4 squares. To work out percentages like these it is often useful to find 10% first by dividing the number by 10. 10% of 20 = 20 ÷ 10 = 2.
13b	16 m^2	1	If the whole garden (20 squares) has an area of 80 m^2 then each square must have an area of 4 m^2. The pond has an area of 4 squares, so $4 \times 4\ m^2 = 16\ m^2$.
14	2M − 14 = 0	1	Subtraction questions can often be described using the words 'less than'. In this case, however, the order that the numbers are read alters, e.g. 10 − 3 is 'Three less than ten'.
15a	$\frac{1}{3}$ or $\frac{2}{6}$ *or* an equivalent fraction.	1	The safari park plan can be divided into 6 equal sections, called sixths. The lion's area covers two such sections (two sixths). This fraction is equivalent to one third.
15b	12 km	1	Children often confuse area and perimeter. The perimeter of a shape is the distance all the way around the edge. If one side of a square is 3 km, then each side of the square is 3 km, making a total of 12 km.

Question number	Answer	Mark	Parent's notes and additional comments
16	0.45, 0.55	1	If children have incorrectly circled 0.98 and 0.2, point out that the column to the right of the decimal point shows how many tenths there are (e.g. when something has been split into ten equal parts). In 0.98 there are 9 tenths. In 0.2 there are 2 tenths. Ask your child to add 9 tenths and 2 tenths and he or she should see that this comes to <u>more</u> than 10 tenths – 10 tenths is the same as 1. Encourage your child, also, to think of 0.2 as 0.20, so it is easier to see that 0.98 and 0.20 do not have a total of 1.
17a	Six more squares should be shaded. These can be made from part squares provided the total number of new squares shaded is 6.	1	This question requires children to either: Know that one quarter is double one eighth (if one eighth is 3 squares, one quarter is 6 squares) *or* Find one quarter of 24 by dividing 24 by 4.
17b	$\frac{9}{24}$ or $\frac{3}{8}$ *or* an equivalent fraction.	1	
18a	270°	1	The turn clockwise from 3 to 12 involves three right angles (90°). $3 \times 90 = 270$.
18b	5	1	Each 90° turn can be split into three equal parts, e.g. from 3 to 6 on the clock the hand will turn 90° in total. So from 3 to 4 it will turn 30°, and from 3 to 5, 60°.
19a	Jo	1	On the graph, there is 1 missing from the Drink column, 0 missing from the Roll column, 2 missing from the Chocolate column and 1 missing from the Crisps column. This is what Jo had in her lunchbox.
19b	Award a mark for any explanation that refers to reading the graph and looking at the table and counting – even if the answer to question 19a is wrong.	1	
20	2 m Award one mark for workings that show an attempt to multiply 20 cm by 9, $9\frac{1}{2}$ or 10, even if the answer is incorrect. Award one mark if the answer is given in centimetres, i.e. 200 cm.	2	The total number of bricks used to make the wall is $19 + \frac{1}{2} + \frac{1}{2} = 20$ bricks. Regardless of where the half bricks are placed, this means there are a total of 10 bricks in each row. 10×20 cm = 200 cm = 2 m

Answers

Test B

Question number	Answer	Mark	Parent's notes and additional comments
1a	147	1	
1b	31	1	Children often attempt questions of this type using trial and error, e.g. trying to multiply 17 by different numbers to get 527. This involves a great deal of time. Instead, encourage your child to see that multiplication questions can be rearranged to make division questions, e.g. $2 \times 5 = 10$ and $10 \div 2 = 5$. Here children should divide 527 by 17 to get 31.
1c	Any division question with an answer of 12, e.g. $12 \div 1$, $24 \div 2$, $36 \div 3$, $240 \div 20$.	1	
2	82, 18	1	
3a	£305.80 Do not award a mark for the answer £305.8 or £305.80p	1	Money answers must be written correctly for questions of this type. Calculator questions like these are often selected to see whether children can interpret the display in the context of money. Amounts of money should never be written with both the **£** sign and a **p** sign
3b	72 Award one mark for the answer 71.9 or 71.942446.	2	Children need to divide £500 by £6.95 to find the least number of hours. This, however, does not give a whole number of hours and children must round this number up to the next nearest whole number, i.e. 72.
4	78 mm	1	
5	 One mark can be awarded for 	2	Children can use tracing paper or a mirror for questions such as these.
6a	$\frac{1}{6}$	1	Children should notice that there are 6 cards and that one of the cards is from Granny. Thus the probability is one out of six. Probabilities generally can be written in words or as fractions or decimals, e.g. **one out of four, $\frac{1}{4}$ or 0.25**
6b	$\frac{1}{2}$ Award one mark for $\frac{3}{6}$	2	Children should notice that there are 6 cards and that three of the cards are from men. Thus the probability is three out of six. To give a fraction in its simplest form, divide the top and bottom numbers of the fraction by the same number, in this case 3.
7	Any of the following answers: −5, 1 −4, 2 −3, 3 −2, 4 −1, 5	1	

Question number	Answer	Mark	Parent's notes and additional comments
8	Glasgow	1	192 + 210 = 402 miles
9a	8.30 and 9.00	1	
9b	120°C Award a mark for any answer within the 118°C–122°C range.	1	Show children that each 50 is split into 2 sections, so each must be worth 25.
9c	150 minutes	1	If your child has answered $2\frac{1}{2}$ hours, show him or her that the question asks for the answer in minutes.
10	21 Award one mark for workings containing the number 7, with an incorrect answer.	2	This is a ratio question. Each team has 2 boys. If there are 14 boys altogether there must be 7 teams. If there are 7 teams, each with 3 girls, there must be 21 girls.
11a	57 × 7 = 399	1	Here children should find which single-digit number would divide exactly into 399 with no remainder. This number is 7. To find the two-digit number, divide 399 by 7 to get 57.
11b	450 ÷ 5 = 90	1	
12	133 cm Award one mark for workings that show an attempt to add 180 and 86 and divide by 2, or find the difference between 180 and 86 and to divide by 2, with an incorrect answer.	2	
13a	C	1	An isosceles triangle is a triangle with two equal sides and two equal angles.
13b	D	1	A regular shape is a shape with equal sides and equal angles.
13c	A	1	
14	495	1	To find $\frac{5}{8}$ of 792 with a calculator, divide 5 by 8 and multiply by 792.
15	6 Award one mark if working shows an attempt to divide 425 by 75 with the answer 5.6666.	2	It does not make sense to have bought 5.6666 Merry Meals. Children must round up the answer to the nearest whole number.
16	21	1	Children often attempt questions of this type using trial and error, e.g. trying to divide 894.6 by different numbers to get 42.6. This involves a great deal of time. Instead, encourage your child to see that division questions can be rearranged, e.g. 10 ÷ 5 = 2 and 10 ÷ 2 = 5. Here children should divide 894.6 by 42.6 to get 21.
17a	C	1	Children can find it difficult to visualise reflections in a diagonal mirror line.

Question number	Answer	Mark	Parent's notes and additional comments
17b	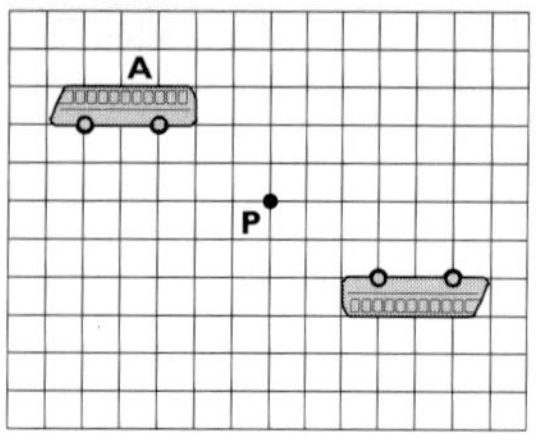	2	Tracing paper can be used for questions of this type.
18	All lines must measure 10 cm. Each angle inside the triangle should measure 60°. Award 1 mark for an angle of 60° (between 59° and 61°) where lines are not 10 cm.	2	Equilateral triangles have equal sides and equal angles. Since the angles inside all triangles add to make 180°, each of the three equal angles is 60°.
19	£34.68	1	17% of 204 can be worked out in the following ways: 17 ÷ 100 × 204 *or* 17 × 204 ÷ 100 *or* 204 × 0.17
20a	1 second	1	
20b	4 seconds	1	After 4 seconds Chloe's stone is 6 m in the air and Andy's is 12 m.
20c	An explanation that the children's hands as they throw the stones will not be at sea level.	1	

Answers

Mental Maths Test

Award 1 mark per correct answer.

1. 90
2. 12
3. 20304
4. three fifths or $\frac{3}{5}$
5. 6
6. 3500 ml
7. 360
8. 19
9. 17
10. 2 m
11. 9
12. 7
13. 16
14. 75
15. $\frac{40}{100}$ and $\frac{2}{5}$
16. Sanjay 29 m
17. 24
18. 5.1
19. £1.06
20. 6, 10, 5

Answers

National Curriculum Levels

Mark scored in Test A	
Mark scored in Test B	
Mark scored in Mental Maths Test	
Total score	

The National Tests are levelled according to the child's total score.

Mark	24 or below	25–51	52–79	80–100
Level	**Level 1/2**	**Level 3**	**Level 4**	**Level 5**

For each test this can be broadly broken down as follows:

Test A	**Mark**	0–10	11–20	21–31	32–40
	Level	**Level 1/2**	**Level 3**	**Level 4**	**Level 5**

Test B	**Mark**	0–10	11–20	21–31	32–40
	Level	**Level 1/2**	**Level 3**	**Level 4**	**Level 5**

Mental Maths Test	**Mark**	0–4	5–10	11–15	16–20
	Level	**Level 1/2**	**Level 3**	**Level 4**	**Level 5**

If your child has achieved Level 5 in Tests A and B and the Mental Maths Test, he or she could try Test C, the Level 6 Extension Paper, on pages 37 to 42.

1 Put these numbers in order of size, starting with the **smallest**.

0.75 0.7 0.07 0.705

1

2 Put these fractions in order of size, starting with the **smallest**.

$\frac{3}{4}$ $\frac{1}{3}$ $\frac{5}{12}$ $\frac{1}{6}$

1

3 Write two fractions, **each greater than zero and less than 1,** which have a difference of $\frac{7}{8}$.

1

4 A boy can choose between 20% of £45.00 or $\frac{3}{5}$ of £20.00.

Which is more and by how much?

1

TOTAL

4

5 174 children enter a competition.
58 of them are girls.

What is the probability of the winner of the competition being a boy?

Give your answer as a fraction in its simplest form.

2

6 Here are pictures of two **square** badges.

The **area** of the smaller badge is **48 cm²**.

The area of the **smaller** badge is $\frac{4}{9}$ of the area of the **larger** badge.

Calculate the **area** of the **larger** badge.

2

TOTAL

4

7 Find the value of **Y** in the equation below.

$$4Y - 7 = Y + 2$$

2

8 Shape A is an isosceles triangle.

Do not use an angle measurer (protractor) for this question.

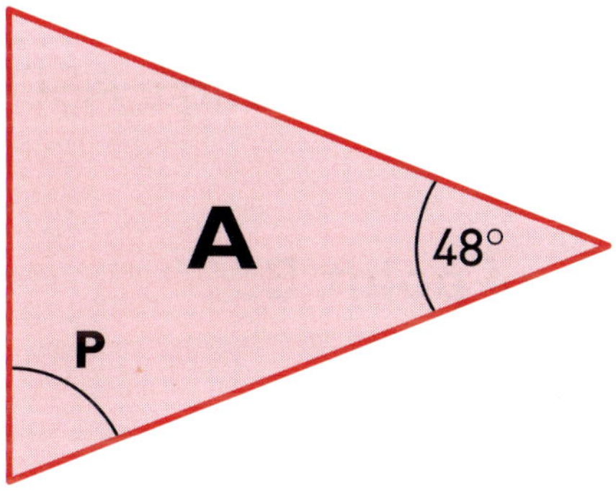

What is the size of angle P?

1

9 In a recipe, the ratio of **sugar to flour** is **2:5**.

A cook makes the recipe using **600 g of flour.**

How much **sugar** does she use?

1

TOTAL

4

10 A triangle has an **area** of **6 cm²** and a **perimeter** of **12 cm.**

Using a ruler, draw this triangle in the grid below.

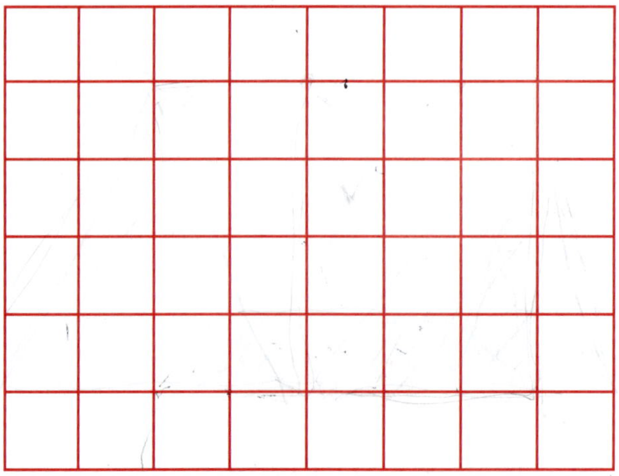

2

11 Two triangles are marked on this graph. Triangle ABD is the reflection of triangle ACD.

Fill in the missing **co-ordinates** of **point B**.

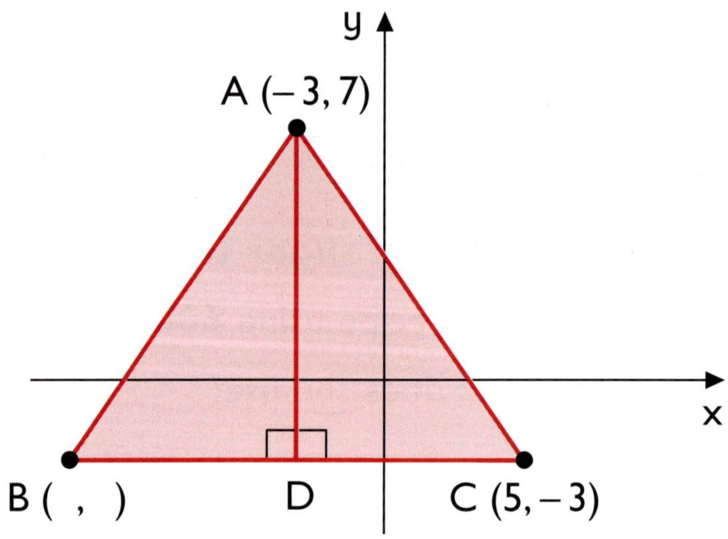

2

Write the co-ordinates of the point exactly half way between A and D.

1

TOTAL

5

12 This pie chart shows different types of holiday accommodation used by a number of families.

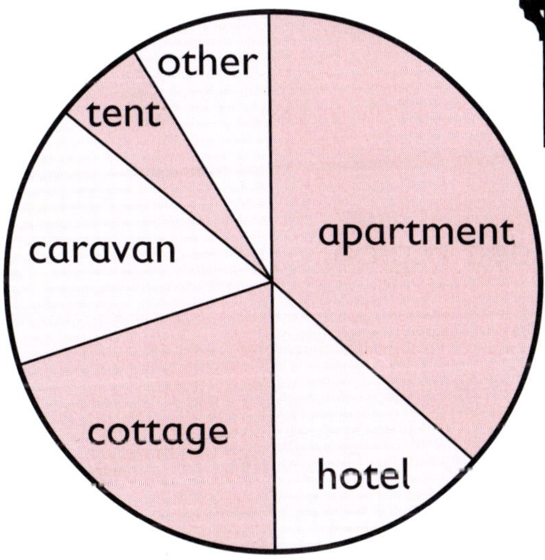

Estimate the percentage of families that used a cottage.

%

1

There were 120 families questioned for this survey.

Calculate the number of families that used a caravan.

You can use an angle measurer (protractor).

2

TOTAL

3

13 A square has sides of **6 cm**. A circle is drawn inside, touching the edges of the square. The region between the edges of the square and the circle is shaded.

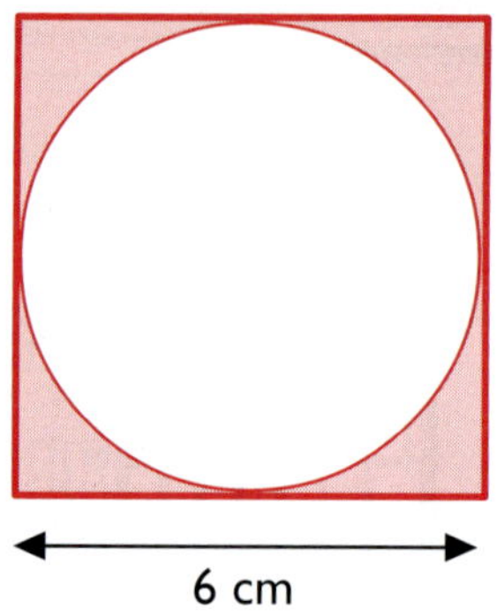

Area of circle = πr^2

Find the area of the shaded region.

cm^2

2

14 Here are some models made from a single layer of cubes.

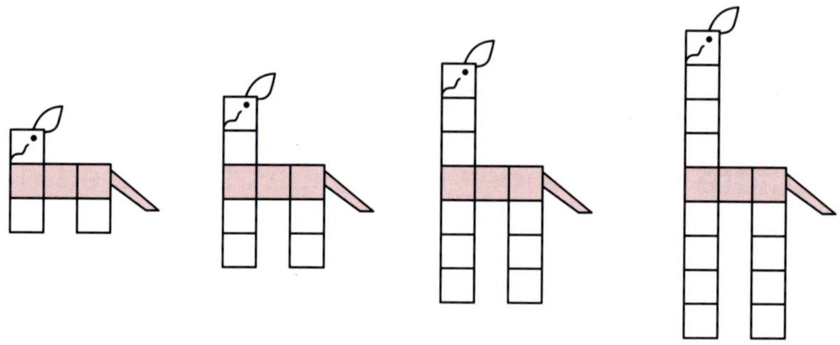

Model number (n)	1	2	3	4	n
Number of cubes (c)	6	9	12	15	?

Write a formula to show many cubes (c) there will be in shape n.

c =

2

TOTAL

4

Question number	Answer	Mark	Parent's notes and additional comments
1	0.07, 0.7, 0.705, 0.75	1	
2	$\frac{1}{6}, \frac{1}{3}, \frac{5}{12}, \frac{3}{4}$	1	Calculators can be used to convert these to decimals if children find ordering decimals easier, e.g. $\frac{1}{6} = 1 \div 6 = 0.1666$ Alternatively, fractions can be changed to equivalent fractions with a denominator (bottom number) of 12, e.g. $\frac{1}{6} = \frac{2}{12}$
3	Various answers possible, e.g. $\frac{1}{16}$ and $\frac{15}{16}$	1	Encourage children to change the fraction to an equivalent form, e.g. $\frac{7}{8}$ to $\frac{14}{16}$.
4	20% of £45 = £9 $\frac{3}{5}$ of £20 = £12. So $\frac{3}{5}$ of £20 is more by £3.	1	Calculators can be used, e.g. $20 \div 100 \times 45$ and $3 \div 5 \times 20$.
5	$\frac{2}{3}$ Award one mark for method showing 174 − 58 = 116, 116 ÷ 174 = 0.666 Or for the fraction $\frac{116}{174}$ or an equivalent.	2	
6	108 cm^2 Award one mark for workings that show $48 \div 4 \times 9$ with an incorrect answer.	2	Children may have incorrectly given an answer smaller than 48, e.g. 21.3 by multiplying 48 by $\frac{4}{9}$. Show your child that 48 is the area of the smaller square.
7	Y = 3 Award one mark for workings that show an attempt to collect Ys on one side of the equals sign and numbers on the other.	2	Possible method: 4Y − 7 = Y + 2 Add 7 to both sides: 4Y = Y + 9 Subtract Y from both sides: 3Y = 9 Divide both sides by 3: Y = 3
8	P = 66°	1	
9	240 g	1	sugar to flour 2 : 5 ? : 600 g 600 g ÷ 5 = 120 g 120 g × 2 = 240 g 240 g : 600 g
10	Triangle with area 6 cm^2 and perimeter 12 cm, e.g sides 3 cm, 4 cm, 5 cm. Award one mark only for an area of 12 cm^2 but an incorrect perimeter or vice versa.	2	
11a	B = (−11, −3)	2	
11b	(−3, 2)	1	

Test C Answers

Question number	Answer	Mark	Parent's notes and additional comments
12a	20%	1	
12b	19 Award one mark if workings show an attempt to divide 57° by 360 and then multiply by 120, or similar method, but with an incorrect answer.	2	Children can answer this question using any of a range of methods.
13	8 cm^2, *or* 7.7 cm^2 etc. Award one mark for attempts to find area of square = 36 cm^2 and area of circle = approx. 28.3 cm^2, but with an incorrect answer.	2	Area of a circle = πr^2 radius (r) = $\frac{1}{2}$ diameter diameter = 6, so r = 3 $\pi r^2 = \pi \times 3^2 = \pi \times 9$
14	$c = 3 + 3n$ *or* $c = (3 \times n) + 3$ *or* equivalent equation.	2	

Answers

National Curriculum Levels

Test C	**Mark**	16–24
	Level	**Level 6**

Level 6 cannot be awarded unless an overall mark of Level 5 has been achieved for Tests A and B and the Mental Maths Test.